Objects
Things
Stuff

Messy Bits We Carry Around

Poetry Collection by L.M. Beatty

Objects Things Stuff
Copyright © 2025 L.M. Beatty

DARK THIRTY POETRY PUBLISHING
ISBN: 978-1-0685766-7-6

Beatty, L.M.
First edition

Artwork by L.M Beatty

DTPP38

DARK
THIRTY
POETRY
PUBLISHING

For my mom, Constance.

Table of Contents

Growing Pains   1

Retreat   2

In this Bag   3

History, Your Story   6

Musing No. 5   8

Found I & II   10

On a Whim   11

Can we sit in the corner?   12

Above the Clouds I, II, III   14

Not in Love   15

Dry Cereal   16

Open Call — Closed to Your Submissions   18

A Beautiful Mind   21

Change   23

Away   24

Musing No. 4   26

Scars   27

Complaint No. 1   28

Americana   29

Scent of success   32

Off Line I, II, III & IV   33

Flex ability   36

Breath Held   38

Berry pie   39

Visionary   42

Sun glass   44

Tension I, II & III   45

Bedfellows   47

Full   49

On view   50

Permanence   51

Simply Arranged   53
AWAKEN   54
Complaint No. 2   55
Friendship   57
Unequally Yoked   59
Anyone & Everyone   61
Musing No. 3 (Bemused)   63
Weapons [words, pen in my pocket]   65
Hope   67
We knew   69
The blessing   70
Flash light   72

Growing Pains

When moms don't answer phones
Somehow
It adds insult to injury
I'm an adult
I don't need to be parented
I just
Need my parent.
She's busy,
Working, gardening, reading, sleeping.
She's an adult.
Adults just have to do things.
I just have to make decisions.
On my own.
But I don't want to.
I just want my mom to pick up the phone.
She trained me well
For adulthood.
I am prepared.
But I'm not ready
For her to not pick up the phone.

Retreat

I don't want this to end.
Funny, because I was dreading its start.
It is hard to allow your heart to just be.
Disengagement takes time,
one must unplug to be able to fully reset.
Dial down the action and turn up the silence.
What do you hear when you're totally still?
Emotions boil up as memories flood in—
all that remains is your heartbeat, your breath.

In this Bag

In this pliable, foldable, wearable bag
I place a semi-confident assumption
that I will be ok.
I accept its quirks as I hope it accepts mine.
In this bag, I hold snapshots of the past
and consider future plans.

For as much as this bag is meant to carry all
of my knicks and knacks,
it can't quite contain the mass of my emotions,
the weight of my anxieties,
the expectations of my dreams.

But just when I think I can't add anything else,
my bag magically expands—
allowing me to take up a bit more space in the world.

In this bag I've made a home.
In it I dump: objects, things, stuff—
those messy bits we carry around.
With this bag, I press on with life.
I may not always know
where I am headed,
but I know I'll always have room
to tote around what I need
for each moment.

My work accompanies me,
as do my notebooks full of creative scribbles.
With my bag, I never lack for things to do.
Even while riding the train

or sitting on a park bench—
waiting for nothing, for something—
I can hold my bag.
I fidget with the smooth leather buckle,
wind my fingers again and again with the scarf.
I hug my bag close to my chest.
There's comfort in its fullness,
in the knowledge that what lies within
will sustain my day.

Snacks, sunglasses
tumble forth if I'm not careful.
Pens, discarded candy wrappers
tangle together in a productive jumble.
My wallet within holds
lip balm and credit cards,
stamps and hair ties,
gum and tampons,
bandages and cash.
A mini bag in and of itself;
a lifeline in life's emergencies.

My bag may appear to be
a big black hole of curious confusion,
but it actually keeps my life
neatly organized and on the move.
Hand grasping the handles,
zipper pulled tight,
I'm grounded and ready
for whatever may come—
well, almost.

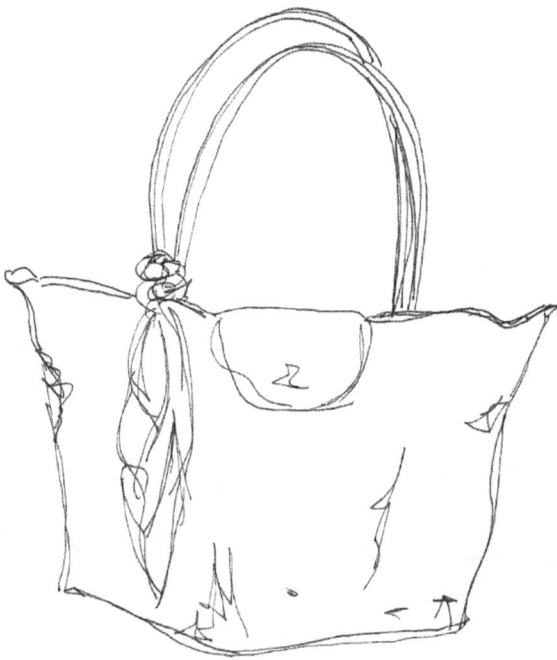

History, Your Story

Love the story you're living right now.
In a not-too-distant future, you'll see its beauty;
you'll have learned a few of its lessons.

The story of your present frames you in the role
of the main character. Please rise to the occasion.
Only you are suitable to fill the position.

The plot will evolve as only good stories can
with gentle turns and jarring twists. You will
laugh, cry, fail, succeed.

The setting may shift beyond what your imagination
can conjure. But isn't there some peace in being
wholly unable to accurately predict exactly where
you might go?

You are not alone. The other characters will drift
around and near you. They'll be full of mixed
measures of love, support, jealousy, pride.

Only you have control of your own actions
and reactions. You cannot manage other people's
expectations. But, you can forgive and show empathy.
You can loyally show up and genuinely play your part.

The story you are living right now is lovable
because, by design, you are loved.
The story you are living right now is valuable
because you are inherently worth a million happy endings.
The story you are living right now is exciting

because there's no way to know
what will happen
in the next chapter.

The story you are living right now has purpose
because you are still living.

History is your story.

Musing No. 5

Fact:
By nature, I avoid toxic habits.
Confession:
I've always wanted to be a smoker.
But not smell like one
or have ill health effects.

There's just something romantically sophisticated
about taking a long deep draw on a cigarette
before blowing out a smooth curl of smoke.

I think, perhaps,
what I actually want
is to feel my breath.
To see the pull and push—
my life incarnate.

I've smoked exactly one cigarette
in my entire life.
I loved it.
Which is why I never bought my own carton;
why I've never started the habit.
I don't think I would quit if I made it a practice.
Instead, I somewhat begrudgingly
practice yoga.

Probably why
I love doing yoga
is precisely my compulsion to smoke.
The breath—
the focus on the in and the out;

the rise and the fall;
the tension and release.

I unroll my mat with regularity
similar to that of serious smokers.
I rinse my toxins out
as others inhale them in.

We can all agree:
Yoga is better for the body.
And yet,
I still wish I could more viscerally
feel and see my breath.
Casually slinging a slim white cylinder
between my fingers as true artists do.
I want to feel the weight
of my life's presence;
to watch it fade away into the ether,
swirling into oblivion.

Found I & II

I. Someone lost their sterling silver turquoise ring:
a chunky piece of metal and rocks
evoking the sea or the mountains or pure beauty.
A ring can be removed as can the memory
of where it was placed—both a small afterthought.

I found the ring, but not the owner.
One person's cast off, another's treasure.
It's in my safekeeping now;
securely surrounding my right middle finger.
Once, I lost it while shopping;
its absence cut viciously
across my bare finger and up to my heart.
Now I never take it off—it's part of who I am.
Carried through each day as a reminder
that there can be joy beyond loss; for me, for others.

II. I lost the poem which had a profound impact on my
creative journey. For 15 years I searched to no avail,
yet it lingered in my brain; the words just out of reach.
The essence of written magic floating around my mind.

Ironically, the poem spoke of tattoos.
Those inky lines of permanence faded by time
yet still marked in my mind with a distinct impression.

I finally found the poem in a book on a shelf
in an art gallery on a trip to Oman.
Refreshed now in my memory, I let myself lose it again.
That poem had nothing to do with that place,
but everything to do with me.

On a Whim

Tick & tock.
Time passes slowly
or sometimes quick.
Waiting for paint to dry.
Looking up,
staring out.
Here I am.
Where I'm supposed to be.

Can we sit in the corner?

I'd really prefer a booth.
I might not tell you that
because it's hard to articulate
exactly how vulnerable
I feel at a table.
Can we sit in the corner?
That would really be
my preference.
I'll face the room
so I can keep track of the people.
I promise I won't
be distracted
by the movement.
But I will be aware of any threats.
I'll protect you
unlike how things went
for me.
A table is fine, some days.
But I would rather
keep my back to the wall.
That way,
no one can sneak up
from behind.
If we sit at a booth,
I can fully relax.
I'll be more present,
I promise.
I will be able to focus
on the future
instead of being dragged back
into a painful past.

Above the Clouds I, II & III

I. Let me be above the clouds
just for a moment;
up here, I can breathe.
The worries of the earth have to leave me alone.
I can't tend to my garden above the clouds.
I can only dream of the roses, peonies & lilacs
that will make my home a glorious altar to the senses.
I can't harvest my vegetables.
I can only wonder at the memory or the prospect of a meal
crafted with love to nourish family & friends.
I can't survey the disasters of flood & famine, wrath or war.
For better or worse, I can only float in peace.

II. Sometimes, I desire that my view of the heavens
would be unobstructed by the breadth of my wings.
I could fly totally free & untethered.
But, it's the sight of the wings that centers me;
reminds me of my duty on the ground.

III. For it is not yet my time to live above the clouds.
I'm merely a transient visitor, temporarily exploring
a realm I can't yet fully comprehend.
The sun, moon & stars prefer that I should descend,
that I might better appreciate the dulled shine
of their far-off beauty.
For it is not my place to concern myself with great matters
or things too wonderful for me.

So, let my soul soar above the clouds
as my feet rest sure & rooted on the ground.

Not in Love

Reflection
Returned or not, love.
The calling is set, reveal
your heart, your home—joy.

Response
Will I unsee the best in those who love
to cherish most my own unhappy thoughts?
For how can I in jealous space create
a boundless *joy de vivre*? It cannot be.
This must be changed. I must cast off all doubt
that love is something to be found. In truth:
l'amour unrequited breaks hearts in haste.

A boundless love comes forth in strands of sun,
with bright and bold warmth to a friendly face.
It seeks only to heal, to help, to save,
un trêsor so pure, a genuine gem.
I will be a lover to have, to hold,
for friends and foes I'll shine and make merry.
Share I must this happy crown—*Reine de Coeur.*

Dry Cereal

I'm in a rush.
There's only time
for dry cereal
black coffee
too hot then suddenly tepid.
My schedule dictated
by a paper diary,
a digital calendar,
a note in my phone.
I can only hope
they all align.
Slave to the to-dos
I wander like a zombie
day in
day out
hoping I did
what I should
regardless of what
I realistically could.
Munching aimlessly
on dry cereal;
pretending it's a meal
until sometime
in the distant future
when I can actually sit
and eat
and pause
and breathe
and collapse into rest.
Maybe tomorrow
nourishment will resemble food

more than the empty-calorie phrase
"I'm really busy"
which seems to be
my only response
to "How are you?"
I suppose it could be worse.
At least I had time, money, energy,
to buy some cereal.

Open Call – Closed to your Submissions

"Open call for poetry,"
the zines & mags announce emphatically.
"We want you, we need you,
trust us with your words."
They aren't lying, they aren't false,
but the actual requirements tell a skewed story;
dry prose in small print which dulls your dreams
and drags you back into reality.
It is unlikely that you,
the writer of poetry,
will be a poet.

For it is impossible to be a poet.
Hard enough to write poetry;
damningly difficult to produce, promote, please & price
those raw crumbs of your unearthed soul.

You might think
that to be a poet,
one must simply write poetry & claim the title.
There is no official gate that prevents you
from finding the success you seek.
Unfortunately, you are naïve.

To be a poet necessitates endless conquests
of your own mind and others' hearts.
The crusade is long & lonely.
To be a poet requires much sacrifice and yields little gain.
One must be comfortable resting in the doldrums,

ready to jump to attention in the crest of a wave.
Ideas flood the brain but coherent thoughts come
in the inconsistent trickle
of the end of a thunderstorm.
There until they're not.

To be a poet is to be a contradiction.
Poetry must be timeless & relevant—
created in a vacuum & stored in a vault;
erased of traces of inspiration
until a themed call warrants
thumbing through archived phrasing,
hoping to find an aged thread of relatable content
to weave a new tapestry of captivating storytelling.

To be a poet means shameless exposure of self.
Promote your accolades
but don't share the associated work.
Curate your essence to yield engaged supporters
but guard your content as raw, precious gems—
yet to be assessed—debatably holding value.
If you dare to post publicly, make the debut count,
but understand only your meager following
will see the doomed release of your genius.
The elite won't publish poems tainted
by the enjoyment of the common people.

To be a poet requires action & platform.
Stand on your box of soap
to loudly expound on your narrative of the world.
Your words should be fresh but not clean;
written with abandon but restrain it into
recognizable shapes;

scrubbed into stark minimalism
still possessing maximum potential for impact
on the ambiguous masses.
Don't be safe, don't be lovely,
don't be soft, don't ever stop—
the people desire a steady stream
of your wild consciousness.
Don't forget:
you owe your inner being to the faceless scroll.

To be a poet, to be an artist, to be creative
is to be controversial.
The edge in your voice may be as sharp as a sword
or dull as a butter knife, but to be taken seriously
you must have that inherently ill-defined *je ne sais quoi*.
Don't write what you want if you want to be published.
Write what you think "they" want.
Consider your commercial viability.
Be ready to defend your creativity at every turn.
Articulate your inherent worth in five single-spaced pages.

To write a poem is a humble cause.
To collect your poetry is an honored pursuit.
To share your work is mist & shadow.
Often critiqued,
frequently misunderstood,
rarely accepted—
endless rejection.

To be a poet is possible,
just be sure to read the small text
if you ever want to see your words in print.

A Beautiful Mind

I need to beautify my brain.

I don't often let her take up intentional space.
She thrives on the autopilot I've programmed her for.
Routine.
Repetition.

But lately, I've given her space for ideas to take root—
a dangerous plan for an unexplored landscape.

Over silent lunches punctuated only
by my chomping sounds as I
methodically chew my salad,
or in the steamy confines
of a too hot shower,
I bask in the weightiness of my brain.

She is laden with the burdens of the world,
bogged down by the heavy rains of grief.
There are holes where I have to dig hard
to recall memories of the not so distant past.
And yet,
there are lovely spots of restoration
where gouged flesh healed over with new growth—
redeeming painful traumas.
She may not be beautiful in the conventional sense,
but I know she is full of lovely potential.

Though it doesn't always come naturally,
I must cultivate a sense of goodness.
I need to nurture positivity, not just in thoughts

of myself, but in how I view others, the world.
I want my mind to flourish amidst the thorns,
bloom beyond a tangle of rotted roots.

I will consciously continue to beautify my brain
so that my subconscious can be a sunny place
of grace and generosity of spirit.
Then, in quiet moments of reflective solitude,
the garden of my mind will be at peace.

Change

If you sit still as daylight wakes and pause,
expand your lungs with air sweet, full of peace—
moments, time stands still you almost forget
what it was to you, the meaning of life.
And yet in a breath suddenly it's clear:
a life lived well gives forth life abundant.
Such shame to waste a minute. Time's no thief.

The sun the moon the world spin ever on
but how we choose to spend defines true worth.
Life's value hung: measures of love and mirth.
To tip the scale, imagination joins
piled high with a generous heart. To give
of oneself is a precious gift received.
Quality shared, glimpse of magic revealed.

You are pure nature—Divinely-designed,
such beauty contained, bound for movement. Joy!
Such passion destined for sorrow and grief.
Creation created for creation.
Remember today your purpose, your role:
you're needed to nurture; help others grow.
It won't be easy, survival takes grit.
Only requirement: do try your best.
Empty your lungs release expectations
body at rest, soul on fire: you can't lose.

Away

If
I never left
I could not
understand
contentment.
For being
away
is the only
way
to come
home.
Then,
when I stay
and
wait,
the journey
feels
a gift.
Without
one,
I can't
truly
love
the other.
Travel:
'tis
a most
ingenious
paradox.
Cue
the music.

Book
the trip.
Go away.

Musing No. 4

If the Boston fern that my grandma gave me
6 years ago dies,
is that bad juju?

Will I receive 7 years of bad luck?

Will my unborn children have 8 toes?

Will my true love never find me?

Nope, those curses are reserved solely for memes
and Facebook posts.

Even so, I'm doing my darndest to not let my fern fail.
The wrath of a disappointed grandma
may be life's most severe punishment.

Scars

It doesn't take much effort to create
a lifetime of damage; to spoil the perfection
of a smooth façade. But come to think of it:
even before being marred by a weapon
was anything ever without fault? For before
the damage was done, imperfections were imparted.
There is no true symmetry in nature,
there is nothing created by God that doesn't
have a blemish. To exist is to experience pain.
To exist is to endure. Newness requires that
the old be put to rest; discarded peacefully.
We were never destined to stay whole, but
neither were we meant to succumb to the
breaking of our skin or our spirit. So,
grant yourself time & grace. Don't rush the healing.
The body & heart intuitively know
from where to seek help. Give your hurt
some space. Your scars aren't signs
of weakness; they are proof of living resilience.

Complaint No. 1

Are squid that rare?
Or is there just a menu upcharge
for things that haunt our nightmares?
Either way, I don't care to talk about squid.
The last time I ate calamari I almost
convinced myself I had food poisoning.
It actually tasted great but my stomach
didn't want to accept the remains
from my mouth. I didn't throw up,
but I thought about how I might.
On the other hand, I'm always down
to enjoy the grey-blackness of pasta made
from the ink of those 8-legged creatures.
It's extra salty and feels that perfect
balance of wrong and right found in the
delight of late night pizza or early morning
ice cream. There's no reason not to like it.
So, I suppose, there's no reason not to like
squid. They are mythically inspiring
sea dwellers whose sole purpose is to
scare the barnacles off sailors and provide
salty and debatably satisfying small bites
that cost too much.

Americana

I used to love America.

She was expansive, she was bold, she was great.

The mythology, the lore didn't hide her faults.
Like all gods, she had stumbled and fallen.
Numerous were her vicious sins,
but many were her stellar victories.
She was scrappy; an ambitious overcomer.
In my naivety, I saw her as a beacon
of what could be good in the world.
As she and I advanced in years,
I hoped for her continued growth in generosity
and I prayed for wise leadership
in her pursuit of peace.

Yet, gradually I noticed a prevailing issue—
America is a construct
of the lofty ideas of failed humans.

"In God we trust."
her people say with a false smile
faintly disguising ulterior motives
and menacing advances.
The deceit was overtly draped
in Stars and Stripes;
curious icons for a nation
now characterized by its disunion.

We hoped that the establishment
of the land of the free

and the home of the brave
would be enough.
We didn't think we would have to
work the land
or take care of the home.
In a country built almost completely
by ambitious immigrants
we constructed barriers
to their future success.
In "god" we trusted.
We the people are that god.

America failed us.
She knew she would.
Our crimson blood continues to overflow
through bullet holes
as the talk of the town
centers on the spectrum of whiteness
in one's skin.
History has repeated itself
'til blue in the face.
The colors that were meant to embrace
bravery, innocence and justice
do little more
than divide us across aisles
and make us squirm in our seats.

So, what now?
What do you do with a country
that inflated itself so much
the balloon popped
into one thousand depressing pieces?
What do you do with a country

that stretched itself so thin
the rubberband of empathy snapped?
What do you do with a country
that doesn't know how to get better,
it only knows who to blame for its sickness?

We can't look back at history,
there are too many accusing fingers
pointing right back at us.
We can't use our resources now
because we can't agree to whom they belong.
We can only look forward
and pray for an authentic spirit of unity.

In God I trust. May He heal the heart of America.

Scent of success

Can you smell it:
the scent of success?
It fills my nostrils
with one (sometimes two)
spritzes of "freedom,"
dabbed on the ridge of my collarbone,
swiped across the tender
skin on my wrists.
I walk out feeling confident
that all who come near
will smell my success
before they even see me.
It's hard to outdress anxiety,
but easy to cover up the musk
of self-consciousness
with an intoxicating perfume.

Off Line I, II, III & IV

I. Lines are important.
They provide boundaries and create structures.
Boundaries are healthy. Without boundaries:
I might overstep, might overwork, might overshare.
Structures hold me up.
With structures: I can thrive, I can rest, I can stand strong.

What's kind of funny is
when people think of "lines" they think:
Level, straight, vertical, horizontal, diagonal.
But the thing is, that really limits the potential of lines.
That really limits the potential of success.

When we were little and told to color,
we recognized that lines come in a variety of forms:
Curved, crooked, wavy, wonky, bold, broken.
All were valid in our eyes.

Yet as we grow,
we increasingly look for the stability of a smooth line.
The small crevices of a looped curve are annoying.
The peaks and valleys of a zigzag are disruptive.
The crests and troughs of a wave are disorienting.

II. I've always liked lines.
I respected their authority.
From elementary hallways,
to choreographed spaces,
to journal entries,
I was happy to follow the lead of the line.

Even now,
I try to stay in line,
on and offline.
I have boundaries. I have structure.
I stay the course,
hoping to achieve my goals
in a linear fashion.

III. A line can be dangerous.
We use it to categorize that which we like
against those we don't—
writing our choices horizontally
on either side of a vertical line.
Division is the cross we choose to bear,
yet we don't do it very well.
It would be better to stand in a line
encircling the world in love.
Handshakes and hugs
dashed streaks of strength.
Looped apologies dotted with kindness.

IV. Nothing is (or can be) perfectly flat,
and that is bothersome.
At my core I desire
the secure boundary of a wall
and the structure of a floor.
But, I've learned to enjoy the space
of an unruly life that respects lines
without worrying
whether they will wander off of the page.
The physical expanse gives me courage
to dream, think and act outside of the box
of societal conventions.

Lines give me hope
that though today is shaky,
tomorrow might level out.

Flex ability

How far can you bend without breaking?
At what point can you no longer stand straight
before starting the inevitable dance
of weight awkwardly shifted side to side.
Where do you feel pain points,
restrictions, tight knots of tension,
muscles pulled taut?
What causes you to hunch over—
pulled down by the weight
of a broken world?
When will you snap—
pushed beyond your limits
with a painful yelp
and an embarrassing display
of the worst version of you?

The older we grow
the more we feel our limitations.
It's harder to touch our toes,
to turn right and left
without getting stuck uncomfortably
in the "wrong" direction.
We ache and groan and wistfully remember
days of our youth—
when life was simplified into right and wrong;
when it didn't matter how much gravity
pulled us down,
we were ready to spring upward.

To maintain agility
into our golden years,

we must flex our abilities.
We must continue to challenge
our core foundations.
We must keep strengthening
our joints, alert our brains, nourish our souls.

Breath Held

Breath held
Bound in a panic
Count my heartbeats
Timed to the song

Of a new voice
Constant in rhythm
Singing sweetness
I've never felt

Inhale
Paused for a moment
Can't remember
Life before now

Breathe out
Saved by a whisper
Found new love; don't
Fall to the ground

Berry pie

Once upon a time,
an old hag of a cookbook
rather rudely informed me that I was not
to be considered ready for marital relations
until I mastered pie dough.
To say that I was shocked by that assaulting
demand is an understatement.

As if I, an unwed almost-spinster,
was not bummed enough
to be making my first pie
for a Thanksgiving feast at which
no plus ones would cozy up to my elbow.
Now, there was published pressure
(and implied judgment).

Or maybe, this was the key to the mystery
of why I was still single!
I didn't need to online date or hang out
at random bars or slide into the DMs
of old college crushes—
I just needed to bake a scrumptious pastry!
"Easy as pie"—say some. But as it turns out,
there has been nothing easy for me regarding pie
(or dating).

Bolstered by adrenaline,
renewed hope in the conditional promise
of "happily-ever-after,"
I cut in the cold butter,
sprinkled ice water,

threw in a pinch of salt,
kneaded the lightly-floured surface
and lovingly wrapped my slightly sticky
ball of soon-to-be flaky dough in cling wrap
to chill in the cold, dark recesses of the fridge.
Kind of.
Mostly, I complained to anyone in earshot of the kitchen
how difficult the directions were to follow,
how hard it was to create an ambiguous consistency,
how frustrated I was at life, at love.

But you know what?
I produced a pie. Rustic for sure,
but it exited the hot oven
golden, crisp and bubbly from its nap.
The berries were bursting
with the sweetness of summer,
seasoned with cinnamon, enhanced by sugar,
bringing warmth to a cold holiday evening.

I stared in wonder at what I had produced.
It looked like a pie,
smelled like a pie,
even tasted like a pie.
Success! And yet, failure.
I still didn't have a beau
to romantically feed—
sweet bite by sweet bite.

Alas, some years later,
I have not had the fortune to find
a charming prince to whom I may present
the bountiful dowry of fresh-baked berry pies.

I scowl in the general direction of the tattered tome
each time I pass the bookshelf.

Perhaps I should be more grateful,
I can now proficiently make pie dough.
Perhaps that archaic cookbook,
should just be burned at 375 degrees Fahrenheit.
Perhaps I will not marry.

Not every fairy tale has a happy ending.
But mine does, because it ends
with a dang good berry pie.

Visionary

Out of focus.
Things seem fuzzy
but are they actually?
My eyes are supposed to
sharpen the shapes
but sometimes they fail—
I get distracted.

What am I even looking at?
Where am I trying to focus?
What am I missing?
Who is getting in my way?
How am I supposed to see
the greater picture
when I can't even
narrow my gaze onto
what is directly in front of me?

Is this really a vision issue?
Is my sight the problem,
or are my viewing troubles
coming from my mind
or my heart
or my spirit?

Have I unintentionally put
rose-colored lens on
to distort things?
Have I intentionally put
blinders on to be willfully
ignorant of what surrounds me?

Have I closed my eyes to opportunities?
Has my blinking become a distraction?

Oh may my sight be restored!
May my focus be adjusted.
May I look forward and behind and around
so I can become truly oriented
to this space in which I exist.
May my vision be for good—
not just in my eyes
but in the sight of the world.
May my perspective shift
to worry less about what is unseen
and to enjoy more of what is.

Sun glass

Both reflective & emissive;
the slim pane pushes away
as much as it pulls in.
Protected by a tint,
luminous façade of deep green,
the color casts a gentle sheen
across the landscape.
My sensitive eyes protected
against an aggressive glare;
ironically blinded by the darkness
meant to soften the blaze.
Windows to the soul
covered by a golden frame
which emulates rays
cast by a turbulent sun.

Tension I, II & III

I. Hold the tension, don't just talk about it.
Don't run from it; walk the line.
We can't be so consumed
by whatever may or may not happen,
by the order of action steps that should happen first.

Yes, society needs to enact change.
Yes, there are constructs that constrict equitable access.
Yes, there are people who will fight
tooth and nail to not fight against injustice.
Yes, there are historical wrongs that must be acknowledged
in the journey to reconciliation.
Yes, there are some (or many) grievances committed
without a shred of remorse.

You cannot right all of those wrongs in one lifetime.
Pick something and do it
with love, respect, grace and truth.

II. Time is not linear. The interwoven nature
of generations of people overlapping their lives
into what we try to frame a society is far more
like a tapestry than it is like a single thread
of your embroidered convictions.

We have woken up, but aren't truly awake.
We live in that ephemeral state between
consciousness and conscientiousness.
It's not enough to know right from wrong.
It is also not enough to find our voice, our call,
and just be loud all the time.

Everything must work together for good.

Most of our days are spent in shadow. As humans
we cannot survive the terrifying splendor of pure
light, nor the awesome depth of total darkness.
We live in a liminal space between the two.
Embrace it.

We are meant to hold that space. For ourselves.
For each other. Our purpose is not
to win, but to ensure that everyone
can thrive.

III. Hold the tension. Firm and strong.
Hold the tension. Though the days are long.
Hold the tension. It's worth the fight.
Hold the tension. We'll shine so bright.

Bedfellows

I can't believe we're here again.

We stare intensely at each other.
But,
we're not actually seeing anything.
There's nothing more to look at,
nothing to be said.
The same story has been told one too many times.
We're caught in a perpetual charade of power dynamics.
Me: thinking I am the master
Him: knowing that he maintains the lead.
Many things are being transmitted across the room.
No words, just the silent void of disappointment for one
and delight for the other.

Communication has never been more clear.
We're engaged again in a battle of wills.
Who will give in first and interrupt the quiet?
I don't want to surrender.
I already threw in the towel.
I refuse to pick it up and wave the white flag.
But,
we can't live like this, nor can we die here;
someone has to make a move.

The longer I look at those big eyes,
the more my heart softens.
I become sympathetic to the cause.
I succumb to the pleading look.
With a deep sigh, I climb in bed.
Immediately he slides over, limb draped across my thigh

I'm coated in the slobber of a sloppy kiss.
My fierce adversary has again defeated me.
Tomorrow I might win the war,
but tonight my victor will enjoy the spoils of a shared bed
and endless ear scratches.
A man's best friend is my greedy bedfellow.
A small price to pay, I suppose, for unconditional love.

Full

There's some pain lacing my joy.
It's woven into every smile and nod.
I can feel the pins and needles
trying to push and nudge me over the edge.
But, I don't give up that easily—
I was born with resilience;
I developed grit;
I gained wisdom;
I earned the opportunity to stand here.

The pain doesn't define me;
the circumstance merely refines my reaction.
I am more than the sum of my broken parts.
I have strength beyond the limits of my tired mind.
I can, and will, press on.
And yet,
the pain follows me there.
Politely I nod and smile,
but internally I grimace and grumble.
Both reactions are valid;
neither more true than the other.

To exist is to experience life to the fullest.
That just happens to include full measures
of mirth and muck;
enthusiasm and ennui;
delight and desperation.
Above all, there's grace for today;
bright hope for tomorrow.
Joy (even laced with pain) is a blessing,
all mine.

On view

Art. My heart,
my soul. You can see—
this is me.

ART. 2025
LMBeatty

Permanence

There's nothing quite so diametrically opposed
    in a world of finites. And yet,
there are few concepts which we both crave
    and fear for the marks it leaves
    on our bodies and souls.
Permanence.

Would love last to eternity and beyond
    as the stories promise us?
Would fame follow us all the way to an end
    where even death wouldn't allow reprieve?
Would wealth carry our dreams and burdens
    through generations with no regard
    for skill or merit?
Would honor give us a worthy seat at every
    table so we could receive endless glory?
Would health keep us strong & supple so that
    never would we miss a memory
    due to illness or ache?

These are ideals, yet we live in a world of ideas;
    a dimension in which the journey matters
    more than the destination.
To achieve permanence would mean
    sacrificing life. Time would be frozen
    and void of connection.
To move and breathe and laugh and cry
    requires fluidity—not just that in a droplet
    of water—but of the tremendous tidal waves
    crashing in the middle of a stormy sea.

We can't find permanence here and, ultimately,
    we wouldn't know what to do with it.
Better to live in the flux. Better to live
    with an open hand.
Let the experiences come and go.

The permanence of forever is somewhere else.

Simply Arranged

This still life—a perfect picture of loveliness,
curated to show the ideal form.
But sometimes, the ideal is actually the ugly:
the worm, the dirt, the decay, the shadow.
For sunlight distinguishes itself
from relative darkness.
There can't be brilliance in life
without the devastation of death.
The two so totally intertwined—
the one magnifies the other.
So it is within the gilded frame of this portrait.
The artist was in full control,
yet yielded to the whims of abundant creativity
to create a masterpiece of genuine distinction.
Beauty is layered into each thick stroke.
Nuance in the subtle shadow;
depth in the fine details—
a complete composition of authentic design.
Joy and pain held in the fine cracks of aged paint.
Once smooth, the canvas now ripples
under the weight of centuries of opinions.
One simple moment captured in a thousand tiny marks.
One million glances cast a lasting impression.

AWAKEN

A night owl, I am. Early birds have to deal with chatty morning
worms that interrupt my precious silence. Even half asleep, I am
astute in finding my bearings in a yet-to-be discovered day. As my brain
kicks on with the bitter taste of hot coffee and blinds flung open,
everything eventually sharpens into focus as I contemplate
newness and the beauty of a fresh start. Blinking slowly, I take flight.

Complaint No. 2

Would you like to leave a tip?
Not really.
I'm already paying a premium price
for not-that-premium coffee
Which I haven't even tasted yet
to know if it's been crafted with excellence.
I haven't been served with kindness.
I didn't have time to use the bathroom
or sit down at a table to notice
their above average cleanliness.
All I've done is walked in the door
and waited a few unnotable minutes in line,
observing the general disinterest
that you and your coworkers seem to have
about your job.
Perhaps you might challenge back
that if I cannot comfortably afford to buy coffee
I should not have even walked in the door.
Perhaps you are correct.
Self-control is hard.
Also, working by myself
for hours alone at home
is quiet and a bit monotonous.
I was craving the white noise
of communal interactions
as much as my brain could use
an afternoon shot or two of dark, creamy energy.
You sigh and barely hide your displeasure.
I awkwardly shuffle
to the end of the bar to await my beverage
and check my bank account.

We're at odds, but not really with each other.
Our battles are vertical, not lateral.
You want more compensation
and possibly, an entirely different career path.
I want a delicious drink in a timely manner
that doesn't cost so much.
Let's remember, we both chose to be here
despite the fact
that none of those circumstances have changed
since last week.
Please don't ask me for a tip,
just because everyone does it these days,
and maybe I'll give you one.

Friendship

The quiet comfort of a friend
warms the soul like a mug of steaming tea;
on a blustery evening brings heat to the body.

A good friend brings the cool breeze
of a perfect spring morning to awaken
your senses to the present day
as they sprinkle joy into your belly
and sunshine into your mind.

A best friend is the perfect salve for a wound
inflicted by mortal enemies or even those
incurred from a glance in the mirror.
The friend often knows
how to protect your heart
better than you do.

The ultimate friend celebrates
your big and small wins
better than the best cheerleader.
They lift you up and share the excitement
of a job well done without
the weight of jealousy bearing down on their heart.

May we all seek to be the friend
that we wish to have.
May we strive to place others above ourselves.
May we know the beauty of friendship
in its best forms and its bountiful treasure.

Unequally Yoked

We did not see eye-to-eye from the get-go.
He was chomping at the bit, moving too close
to another female. I think I was nervous.
Not in a way that was obvious, but we were
close enough that we could hear each other
breathe. The breath always gives me away.

Reluctantly we set off on our scheduled walk
through the forest. The day could not be more
perfect. Bright blue sky with tufts of soft
clouds lazily floating by. Birch and pine trees framing
the view; little summer flowers gracing the path.

But silently we plodded on; impossibly at odds
with one another, although practically strangers.
We had met once or twice before, and I had been
excited for more time together, but he obviously
did not return the feeling. It was soon apparent
that there was little love to be had.

Still, onward we marched. Forward we moved.
I tried to whisper gentle encouragements; smile
to change the mood as we trotted through the time.
But isn't it true that the baring of teeth can be
interpreted as a threat? I think my signals
were misinterpreted. All I saw were large eyes
starring back in vacant disregard.

Finally, we arrived at our planned destination—
Turtle Lake, it was called, but I didn't ask why.
We splashed in the water—together yet separate—

a void of language and expectations.

And then it was time to return. For a while, we seemed
to settle into a rhythmic routine. Both guiding each other
with nuanced shifts. For a few moments I sensed
a glimpse of trust and respect. Perhaps even a tinge
of amiability. But then we'd unsettle. Yet, I refused to let
my perfect afternoon be ruined.

I matched his fiery energy. I pulled back with firmness
when he tried to push forth. He yielded to my tugs
with an occasional toss of his long brown mane.

Perhaps we were too alike, he and me. Neither quite
as tame as we should be. We lead from our hearts
and spurn the ropes. We'd rather run free, alone
with our hopes. Brego, a leader, and me, a queen.

Anyone & Everyone

Anyone can paint a picture.
Unless they don't have a brush, a canvas, a piece of paper.
Anyone can grow a garden.
Unless they don't have land, seeds, a patch of dirt.
Anyone can learn to read.
Unless they don't have a book, a paragraph, a teacher.
Anyone can make dinner.
Unless they don't have a fridge, a stove, some food.
Anyone can get a job.
Unless they don't have experience, transportation,
a clean background.
Anyone can find a place to live.
Unless they don't have credit, recommendations,
a bank account.
Anyone can improve their health.
Unless they don't have access, insurance, money.
Anyone can pursue their dreams.
Unless they don't have free time, creative space,
systems of support.

Anyone can theoretically do anything. But anyone cannot
do everything. And everything is not always available
to everyone.

But, everyone can do quite a few things without quite a lot.

Everyone can share their wealth: smiles, a bite to eat,
a compliment, some time.
Everyone can change the world:
through kindness, love, sacrifice, empathy.

Everyone can be a friend: building trust, demonstrating loyalty, giving respect, asking forgiveness.
Everyone can seek peace.

If everyone did everything they *can* do, I think it wouldn't be quite so hard for anyone to succeed.

Musing No. 3 (Bemused)

Nora worried about her neck. Or so I heard.
I read about her. I didn't actually read what she wrote.
Honestly I've been worried about mine ever since.
Then, I was at the peak of womanhood.
Or so I thought.
Now, am I?
I read an article. Then another. Maybe four more.
Felt good. Felt bad. Felt indifferent.
Hard to keep track.
Lots of thoughts.
Lots of anxiety.
Drew didn't get work done.
That's a relief.
Stopped wearing makeup because I wanted to be
Recognizable.
Alicia did that.
Everyone cheered.
Added some makeup and got lots of personal attention.
Is that real? Are they fake? Am I pretty? Do I care?
Yes.
In fact, I do care very much.
Vanity runs deep.
My skin is thick, but not enough to insulate my mind from
The haters.
Especially not the one that lives in my head.
It's clear.
My skin, that is.
Until it's not.
Am I still going through puberty?
Nope.
Very much matured.

Very much still picking at pesky pimples.
Is my body working for me?
Or am I working for it?
Only time will tell.
I guess it already is.
My poor neck.

Weapons [words, pen in my pocket]

By little effort, a few simple words
rise in me with power to slice, to cut.
Manipulated persuasion, I think,
I say, I tell, I write, ready to pounce.
Balanced on the tip of my tongue, the edge
of a sword that never dulls. Shall I
forfeit that which I feel? The price I pay
for silent restraint equals in measure
costly preservation of how they feel.
If others can scream, why shouldn't I cry?

That's not to say [to write] self-exposure
makes sense on every occasion. Holding
one's breath, one's voice clarifies vision. Feel
the tension, notice intended response.
Start a battle, but can I win the war?
There must be strategy to engage well.
Order my thoughts, before the first strike. This
will draw less blood more understanding so
the inevitable return holds grace.
Death is not the goal. I shall not murder.

But stay, my hand. To what purpose shall I
wound? No victors rise from passionate crimes.
It's not my place to put others in theirs.
Conquered peoples rise with valid vengeance.
I can temper my emotions without
sacrificing my values. Tête-à-tête
with respect is what I now seek. Violence
no longer welcome. The person in front
of my eyes sweetens the bitter taste left

from carelessly typed words. Can we just talk?

I remember the wounded heart. I see
the pain in their eyes; freed from the façade
of a digital fortress that reduced
thinking to aimless anger, soul to slush.
My pen, once my weapon of choice, laid down.
Civil discourse, a much stronger tool than
show of force. We respond well to kindness.
Exchanging smiles is a conversation.
Resolved to be gracious, intent on peace.
I'll try to understand, I hope you can too.

Hope

Whatever path you take, I hope it is one of beauty.
Whenever you pause, I hope you find joy.
Whatever step you take next, I hope you feel courageous.
Whenever you depart, I hope it is after a season of rest.
Whatever guides your way, I hope it is full of truth & grace.
Wherever your feet go, I hope they lead you to peace.

We knew

We didn't know that would be the day we left forever
houses of memories, memories turned bitter;
ash from fires, smoke that will never dissipate.

We didn't know that the sun would burn us,
blind us with the glory of those who spurned our plight
singed by our audacity to fly too high in freedom.

We didn't know that the garbage we gathered
would become our most prized possessions;
glimmering shards of a distorted reflection of what once
was.

We didn't know that the depth of hate could penetrate
through generations, past borders, across the sea.
Boiling blood; brooding vipers ready to strike.

We knew that life was fleeting.
We knew our dreams might fail.
We just didn't anticipate that there could exist
such terrible pain, anger, crimes against humanity.

The blessing

All of our voices
matter.
If one cannot speak those words
without a crinkle across the brow
or a twitch in the shoulders
then equality is not a value of yours
and this blessing is not
for you, for now.

There must be a full acknowledgment
that we are all created, all fallen,
all capable of good, all susceptible to failure,
all worthy of respect, all in need of grace.

Are you ok with that
at the core of your being?

If no, return to the top. Say those words
again and again and again
until they seep down into the roots
of who you know yourself to be.
It's not too late to change your mind
or your heart.
Peace, joy, calm await you.

If yes, allow these words
to gently pour over your life,
from the top of your noble crown,
down to the humble pads of bare feet.

May you be surrounded by a wall of support
May you be abundant in creativity
May you be treated with dignity
May you be protected by wisdom
May you be confident in discernment
May you be loved with wild abandon
May you fully know that you are valued and valuable.

Go, and live this blessing over others.

Flash light

One lonely beam of illumination,
swerving back and forth
back and forth across the path. My toes
chase the weak streak
of light.

Darkness fell, but the moon
already rose,
soon to be followed
by the orange-tinged radiance
of a fiery sun that will never
cease to be.

The flash of my light is as temporary
as the bug bites dotting my ankles,
small glimmers of long days in sweet summer.

A beat of fear pangs my heart. I know
I am one stumble away from a night
of misery. If I fall in the woods
and no one is around,
will my fall to the ground
make any sound?

My pace picks up, but the beam of light
guiding me home remains steady.
Too much time was spent
worrying about what could be. What if
I lived in the present?
What a gift that would be.

In a moment, I have arrived to my house
basking in the fuzzy glow of porch lights
and swarming lightning bugs.
One last look around to take in the sights.
I extinguish the light in my hand.
Breathe in, exhale slowly,
smile with gratitude.

For the light
will always pierce through darkness.
I need not fear.

Acknowledgements

Growing Pains - Originally published in Free the Verse
Change - Originally published in Dark Thirty Poetry
Publishing - Forgotten Fragments of Time
Permanence - Originally published in Dark Thirty Poetry
Publishing - Forgotten Fragments of Time

L.M. Beatty is a full-time creative embracing such titles as artist, author, freelance copywriter, yoga instructor, florist and retail merchandiser. She holds a double major in international business and political science from Olivet Nazarene University and an M.A. in cross-cultural and sustainable business management from the American University of Paris. She lives south of Chicago, but her heart lives in Paris.

RELEASED BY DARK THIRTY POETRY

ANTHOLOGY ONE
THIS ISN'T WHY WE'RE HERE
MORTAL BEINGS
POEMS THAT WERE WRITTEN ON TRAINS BUT
WEREN'T WRITTEN ABOUT TRAINS
CLOSING SHIFT DREAMS
DESIRE
ANIMATE
THESEUS AND I
I DON'T HAVE THE WORDS FOR THIS
CONVERSATIONS BETWEEN THE SUN AND THE
MOON
SLUTPOP
JADED
I'VE BIRTHED AN IDEA OF YOU
BRUISES
CITY GOTHIC
LONG DIVISION
SAY HER NAME
LUMIN
VESTIGES
FALLING IN LOVE LOST
JUGGERNAUT
STIRRING TO LIFE
FORGOTTEN FRAGMENTS OF TIME
THIS BOOK IS NOT ABOUT JAPAN
BEYOND THE DOORS OF A LAST BREATH
CORPORATE
JANE F*CKING EYRE
THE SNAKE EATS ITSELF
THE MOON AND HER CRATERS
NOCTURNAL
BREWING ANXIETEA
FLAT FRONT
ARE YOU HAVING A GOOD TIME YET?
WORDS TAKE SHAPE

ICARUS ISN'T DEAD
FINDING HOME
DARK PEAKS
OBJECTS THINGS STUFF

www.ingramcontent.com/pod-product-compliance
Lightning Source LLC
Chambersburg PA
CBHW071237090426
42736CB00014B/3123